The Church and the Kingdom

THE ITALIAN LIST

The Church and the Kingdom

GIORGIO AGAMBEN

TRANSLATED BY LELAND DE LA DURANTAYE

WITH PHOTOGRAPHS BY ALICE ATTIE

Series Editor: *Alberto Toscano*

LONDON NEW YORK CALCUTTA

Seagull Books, 2018

La Chiesa e il Regno © nottetempo srl, 2010

Translation © Leland de la Durantaye, 2012

Photographs © Alice Attie, 2011

First published in English translation by Seagull Books, 2012

This compilation © Seagull Books, 2012

ISBN 978 0 8574 2 587 4

British Library Cataloguing-in-Publication Data

A catalogue record for this book is available
from the British Library

Designed by Sunandini Banerjee, Seagull Books

Printed and bound by Hyam Enterprises, Calcutta, India

CONTENTS

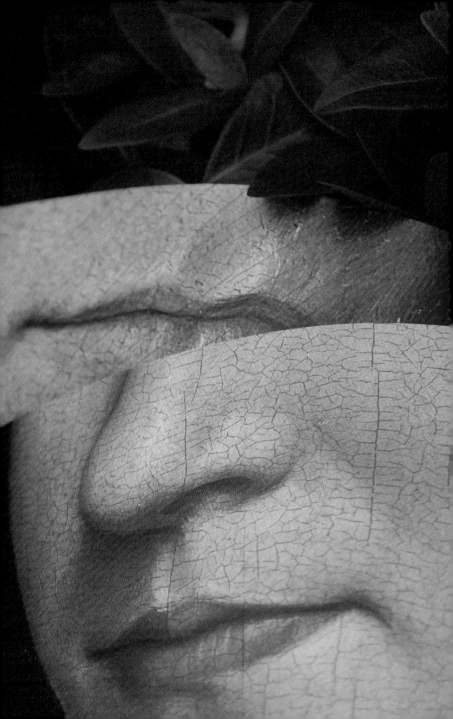

One of the very earliest texts in the ecclesiastical tradition, Clement's Letter to the Corinthians, begins: 'The Church of our Lord sojourning in Rome to the Church of our Lord sojourning in Corinth.' In Greek, *paroikousa*, which I'm translating as 'sojourning', is a term with a very precise meaning. It designates the manner in which foreigners and those in exile dwell. It is opposed to the Greek verb *katoikein*, which designates how a citizen of a city, state, kingdom or empire dwells. This is the formula I've chosen to begin my address to the Church of our Lord, in sojourn or exile, here in Paris.

Why this formula? The answer is because I have come to speak of the messiah. *Paroikein*, to sojourn as a foreigner, is the word that designates how a Christian is to live in the world and, by that token, that person's experience of time—and, more precisely, of messianic time. That in the ecclesiastical tradition this is a technical term, or something approaching one, is clear from the fact, to choose a single instance, that Peter's First Letter (1 Peter 1.17) defines the experience of time proper to the Church as *ho chronos tē paroikias*, and which can be translated as 'parochial time' on the condition that we recall that parish originally meant 'the sojourn of a foreigner'.

It is important to bear in mind that the term 'sojourn' does not refer here to a fixed period of time: that it does not designate chronological duration. The sojourning of the Church on earth can last —and indeed has lasted—not only centuries but millennia without altering its messianic experience

of time. This point requires special emphasis as it is opposed to what is often called a 'delay of the *parouisa*'. According to this position—which has always seemed blasphemous to me—the initial Christian community, expecting as it did the imminent arrival of the messiah and thus the end of time, found itself confronted with an inexplicable delay. In response to this delay there was a reorientation to stabilize the institutional and juridical organization of the early Church. The consequence of this position is that the Christian community has ceased to *paroikein*, to sojourn as a foreigner, so as to begin to *katoikein*, to live as a citizen and thus function like any other worldly institution.

If this is the case, the Church has lost the messianic experience of time that defines it and is one with it. The time of the messiah cannot designate a chronological period or duration but, instead, must represent nothing less than a qualitative change in how time is experienced. For this reason it is inconceivable to speak of a chronological delay in this context as though one were speaking of a train being delayed. Because there is no place in messianic time for a fixed and final habitation, there is no time for delay. It is with this in mind that Paul reminds the Thessalonians, 'About dates and times, my friends, we need not write to you, for you know perfectly well that the Day of the Lord comes like a thief in the night' (1 Thess 5.1–2; 262).[1] In this passage 'comes [*erchetai*]' is in the present tense, just as in the Gospels the messiah is called *ho erchomenos*, 'he who comes'—that is, he who never ceases to come. Having perfectly understood Paul's meaning, Walter Benjamin once wrote that, 'every day, every instant, is the small gate through which the messiah enters.'

I would like thus to speak to you about the structure of this time—that is, of the time that Paul describes in his letters. In this regard, care must be

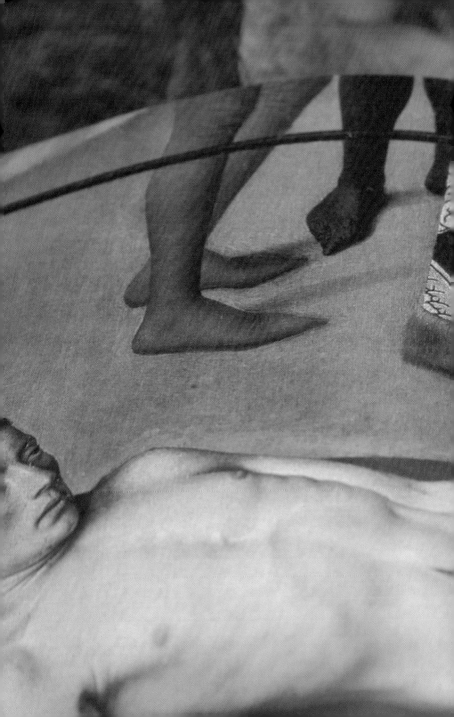

taken to avoid confusion between *messianic* time and *apocalyptic* time. The apocalyptic thinker is found on the last day, Judgement Day. He or she sees the end of time and describes what is seen. If I were to resume in a single phrase the difference between messianic time and apocalyptic time, I would say that the messianic is not the end of time but the time of the end. What is messianic is not the end of time but the relation of every moment, every *kairos*, to the end of time and to eternity. Consequently, what interests Paul is not the final day, the moment at which time ends, but the time that contracts and begins to end. Or, one might say, the time that remains between time and its end.

In the Judaic tradition there is a distinction between two times and two worlds: the *olam hazzeh*, the time stretching from the creation of the world to its end, and the *olam habba*, the time that begins after the end of time. Both terms are present, in their Greek translations, in Paul's Letters. Messianic time, however—the time in which the apostle lives and the only one that interests him—is neither that of the *olam hazzeh* nor that of the *olam habba*. It is, instead, the time between those two times, when time is divided by the messianic event (which is for Paul the Resurrection).

How can we best conceive of this time? If we represent this time geometrically as a segment taken from a line, the definition I've just given—the time that remains between the Resurrection and the end of time—does not seem to present any difficulties. Everything changes, however, if we try to conceive this time more fully. It is perfectly clear that to live in 'the time that remains', to experience 'the time of the end', can only mean a radical transformation of our experience of time. What is at issue is neither the homogenous and infinite line of chronological time (easy to visually represent but empty of all

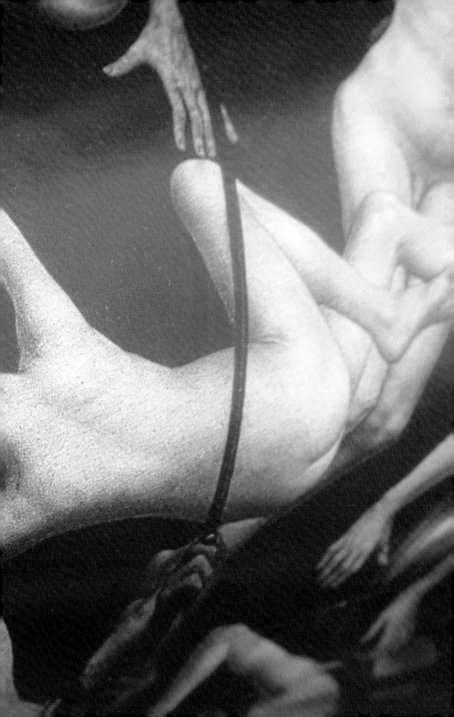

experience) nor the precise and unimaginable instant where it ends. Nor, for that matter, can we conceive of it as that segment of chronological time extending from the Resurrection to the end of time. Instead, what is at issue is a time that pulses and moves within chronological time, that transforms chronological time from within. On the one hand it is the time that time takes to end. But on the other hand it is the time that remains, the time which we need to end time, to confront our customary image of time and to liberate ourselves from it. In the one case, the time in which we believe we live separates us from what we are and transforms us into powerless spectators of our own lives. In the other case, however, the time of the messiah is the time that we ourselves are, the dynamic time where, for the first time, we grasp time, grasp the time that is ours, grasp that we are nothing but that time. This time is not some other time located in an improbably present or future time. On the contrary, it is the only real time, the only time we will ever have. To experience this time implies an integral transformation of ourselves and of our ways of living.

This is what Paul affirms in an extraordinary passage, and which perhaps presents the most beautiful definition of messianic time: 'But this I say, my brothers, time has contracted [*ho kairos synestalmenos esti*—the Greek verb *systellein* indicates both the clewing up of a ship's sails and an animal's gathering of its strength before pouncing];[2] while it lasts, those with wives should be as those who are without, those who weep as though they wept not, those who rejoice as though they rejoiced not, those who buy as though they possessed not, and they that use this world, as not abusing it' (I Cor. 7.29–31; 215).

A few lines earlier Paul had written of the messianic vocation (*klēsis*): 'Let every man remain in the calling in which he was called. Were you called as a slave? Do not be troubled. But if you can become free, make use of it' (I Cor. 7.20–22). The *hōs mē*, the

'as not', means that the ultimate meaning of the messianic vocation is the revocation of every vocation. Just as messianic time transforms chronological time from within, rather than abolishing it, the messianic vocation, thanks to the *hōs mē*, the 'as not', revokes every vocation, at once voids and transforms every vocation and every condition so as to free them for a new usage ('make use of it').

The question's importance stems from the fact that it allows for a proper consideration of the relation between the ultimate and the penultimate, between the last things and the next to last ones which define the messianic condition. Can a Christian live only with the ultimate, only with the last things? Dietrich Bonhoeffer denounced the false opposition of radicalism to compromise for the reason that both options consist in drastically separating ultimate realities from the penultimate ones which make up our everyday human and social condition.

Just as messianic time is not some other time but, instead, an integral transformation of chronological time, an ultimate experience (an experience of the last things) would entail, first and foremost, experiencing penultimate things differently. In this context eschatology is nothing other than a transformation of the experience of the penultimate. Given that ultimate realities take place first in penultimate ones, the latter—contrary to any radicalism—cannot be freely negated. And yet—and for the same reason—the penultimate things cannot in any case be invoked against the ultimate ones. For this reason Paul expresses the messianic relation between final and penultimate things with the verb *katargein*, which does not mean 'destroy' but, instead, 'render inoperative'. The ultimate reality deactivates, suspends and transforms, the penultimate ones—and yet, it is precisely, and above all, in these penultimate realities that an ultimate reality bears witness and is put to the test.

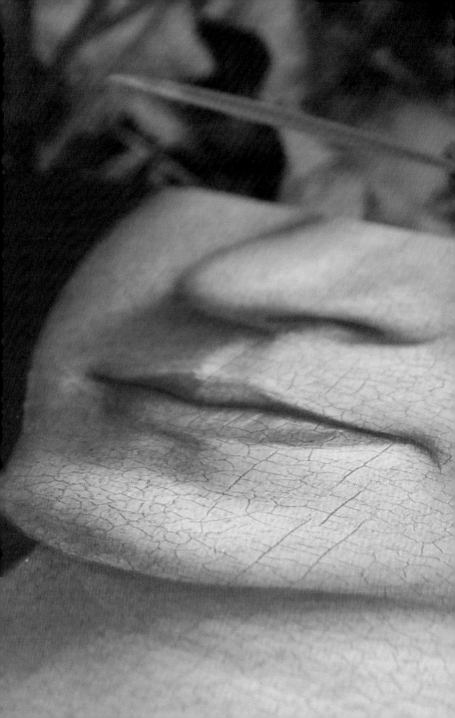

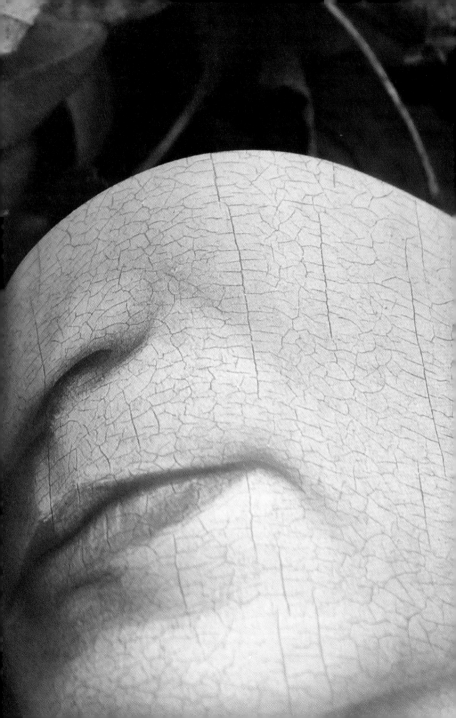

The preceding allows us to understand Paul's idea of the Kingdom. Contrary to the contemporary eschatological interpretation, it should not be forgotten that the time of the messiah cannot be, for Paul, a future time. The expression he uses to refer to this time is always *ho nyn kairos*, 'now time'. As he writes in the Second Letter to the Corinthians, '*Idou nyn*, behold, now is the time to gather, behold the day of salvation' (2 Cor. 6.2; 231). *Paroika* and *parousia*, the sojourn of the foreigner and the presence of the messiah, have the same structure, expressed in Greek through the preposition *pará*: a presence that distends time, an *already* that is also a *not yet*, a delay that does not put off until later but, instead, a disconnection within the present moment that allows us to grasp time.

Living in this time, experiencing this time, is thus not something that the Church can choose, or choose not, to do. It is only in this time that there is a Church at all.

Where do we find such an experience of time in today's Church? That is the question that I have come, here and now, to pose to the Church of Christ sojourning in Paris. An evocation of final things, of ultimate things, has so completely disappeared from the statements of the Church that it has been said, not without irony, that the Roman Church has closed its eschatological window. And it is with more bitter irony still that a French theologian has remarked that, 'Christ announced the coming of the Kingdom, and what arrived was the Church.' This is a disquieting declaration, but one which merits reflection.

Given what I have said about the structure of messianic time it is clear that what is at issue cannot be to chastise the Church in the name of radicalism for its worldly compromises, just as little as it can be to portray the Roman Church—as did the greatest orthodox theologian of the nineteenth century, Fyodor Dostoevski—as a Grand Inquisitor. What is

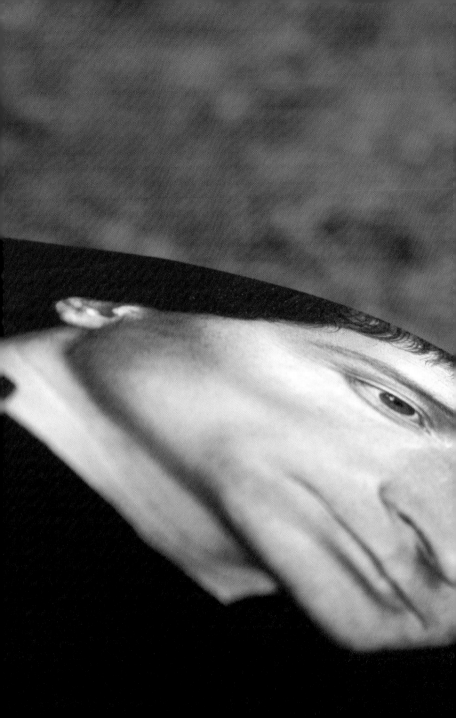

at issue, instead, is the Church's ability to read what Matthew called 'the signs of the times', *ta semeia tōn kairōn* (Mt 16.3; 23). What are these signs which the apostle opposed to the futile desire to know the forms that move across the sky? If the relation of history to the Kingdom is penultimate, the Kingdom nevertheless is to be found first and foremost in that history. For this reason, to live in the time of the messiah means to read the signs of his presence in history, to recognize in the course of history 'the signature of the economy of salvation [*la segnatura dell'economia della salvezza*]'.[3] In the eyes of the Church Fathers—as well as the eyes of those philosophers who have reflected on the philosophy of history, which is, and remains (even in Marx) an essentially Christian discipline—history is presented as a field traversed by two opposing forces. The first of these forces—which Paul, in a passage of the Second Letter to the Thessalonians that is as famous as it is enigmatic, calls *to catechon*—maintains and ceaselessly defers the end along the linear and homogenous line of chronological time. By placing origin and end in contact with one another, this force endlessly fulfils and ends time. Let us call this force Law or State, dedicated as it is to economy, which is to say, dedicated as it is to the indefinite—and indeed infinite— governance of the world. As for the second force, let us call it messiah, or Church; its economy is the economy of salvation, and by this token is essentially completed. The only way that a community can form and last is if these poles are present and a dialectical tension between them prevails.

It is precisely this tension which seems today to have disappeared. As a sense for an economy of salvation in historical time is weakened, or eliminated, the economy extends its blind and derisive dominion to every aspect of social life. Today, we witness the eschatological exigency which the Church has abandoned return in secularized, and parodic form, in the occult sciences that have rediscovered

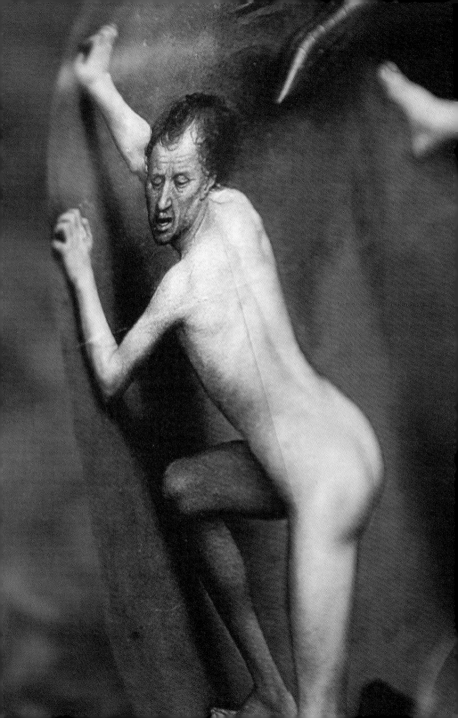

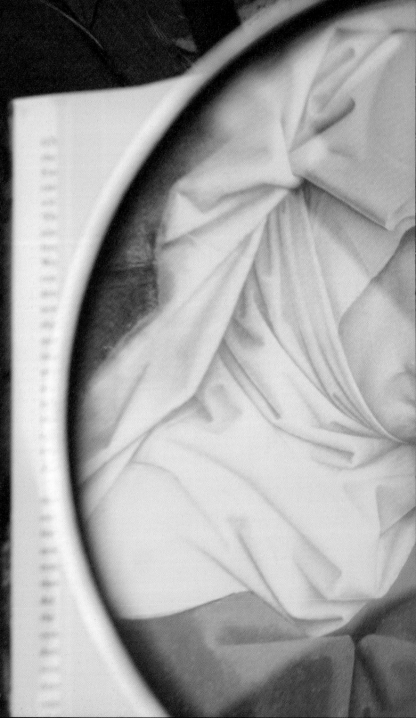

the obsolete gestures of the prophet and announce every sort of irreversible catastrophe. The crises— the states of permanent exception and emergency— that the governments of the world continually proclaim are in reality a secularized parody of the Church's incessant deferral of the Last Judgement. With the eclipse of the messianic experience of the culmination of the law and of time comes an unprecedented hypertrophy of law—one that, under the guise of legislating everything, betrays its legitimacy through legalistic excess. I say the following with words carefully weighed: nowhere on earth today is a legitimate power to be found; even the powerful are convinced of their own illegitimacy. The complete juridification and commodification of human relations—the confusions between what we might believe, hope and love and that which we are obliged to do or not do, say or not say—are signs not only of crises of law and state but also, and above all, of crises of the Church. The reason for this is that the Church can be a living institution only on the condition that it maintains an immediate relation to its end. And—a point which we would do well not to forget—according to Christian theology there is only one legal institution which knows neither interruption nor end: hell. The model of contemporary politics—which pretends to an infinite economy of the world—is thus truly infernal. And if the Church curtails its original relation with the *paroikia*, it cannot but lose itself in time.

For this reason, the question I came here today to ask you, without any other authority than an obstinate habit of reading the signs of the time, is this: Will the Church finally grasp the historical occasion and recover its messianic vocation? If it does not, the risk is clear enough: it will be swept away by the disaster menacing every government and every institution on earth.

Notes

> *The preceding talk—or, perhaps more precisely, homily—was given in the Notre-Dame Cathedral on 8 March 2009, in the presence of the Bishop of Paris as well as a number of other high-ranking Church officials. Its author has lived—or, more precisely, sojourned—in Paris for various periods since the early 1970s.*

1   All Biblical citations are from *The New English Bible with the Apocrypha* (Oxford and Cambridge: Oxford University Press and Cambridge University Press, 1970). At points these have been modified to more closely correspond to Giorgio Agamben's translations from the Greek.

2   It is telling in this regard that English translations have employed various expressions in the attempt to render this difficult phrase, all of which seem to reflect an exceptionally brief chronological period. The King James Bible

uses the expression, 'But this I say, brethren, the time *is* short' and which The Revised Version changes to 'the time is shortened' and The New English Bible modifies to 'The time we live in will not last long.' See *The Holy Bible, Containing the Old and New Testaments* (London and Oxford: Oxford University Press, 1885) and *The Holy Bible: The Revised Version* (Cambridge and London: Cambridge University Press, 1903).

3   The slightly stilted, and slightly obscure, form of this expression is due to the fact that it refers to—or, more precisely, is a luminous abbreviation of—the central ideas expounded in Agamben's two most recent works—*The Signature of All Things* (Luca di Santo and Kevin Atell trans) (Cambridge, MA: MIT Press, 2009) and *The Kingdom and the Glory: For a Theological Genealogy of Economy and Government* (Lorenzo Chiesa trans.) (Stanford, CA: Stanford University Press, 2011).

Afterword:

On Method, the Messiah, Anarchy and Theocracy

LELAND DE LA DURANTAYE

In the preceding discourse Giorgio Agamben
charges the Catholic Church with having forgotten
its calling. He does this not by haranguing crowds
in front of Notre-Dame or nailing theses to its
doors—nor for that matter via newspaper op-eds,
Internet manifestos, Facebook posts or Tweets. Instead, Agamben presents his observations calmly
and courteously *to* the Church *in* the Church.
Notwithstanding this calm courtesy, the charge that
he levels could hardly be graver. It is nothing less

than that the Catholic Church has chosen—over the course of millennia—worldly dominion over its founding ideas and ideals, that it has chosen the consolidation of temporal power over a fundamental experience of time; he charges it with having lost its 'vocation'.

The argument Agamben makes here about the social and spiritual place of the early Church, the evolution of the Church as institution and the conceptions of history and time operative in the Church's founding documents is both lucid and brief enough so as to require no summary here. What do bear noting, however, are two related matters. The first concerns Agamben's idea of method; the second his idea of theology.

Agamben has written some 20 books on topics ranging from aesthetics to politics, poetics to ontology. This diversity of topic is coupled with a unity—albeit an evolving one—of method. This method is one we might call 'philological'. As the brilliant and eccentric art historian Aby Warburg liked to remark, and Agamben has liked to repeat, 'the dear God dwells in the details.'[1] Warburg used this expression as a personal motto and would cite it to colleagues and coworkers at the institute he founded where, many years after his death, Agamben was to study. What Warburg used it to stress was the need for attentiveness to even the most minute details of a work, an idea or an expression in the search for the most fundamental matters. Warburg's at once playful and serious dictum recalls the approach of one of his many admirers—Walter Benjamin—who for his part wrote that to approach the 'truth-content' of a work required 'the most precise immersion into the individual details of a given subject'.[2] Years later, yet another of the thinkers who most shaped Agamben's philological and philosophical approach, Martin Heidegger, wrote in his *Letter on Humanism* that given 'the current penury of the world', we need 'less philosophy and more vigilant thought; less literature and more care for letters'.[3] Such a care for letters marks Agamben's approach, and throughout his work he displays the erudition and precision of a philologist as well as the guiding sense that without investigation of such details true philosophical speculation is impossible.

A clear example of this is to be seen in the first explicitly theological of Agamben's books. *The Time That Remains* (2000) takes the careful form of a patient, precise and phenomenally insightful reading of the first 10 words of Paul's Letter to the Romans. Through a study of that part—Paul's incipit— Agamben presents not only the whole of that letter, and not only the whole of Pauline thought, but also the matters that most interest him in *The Church and the Kingdom*: Paul's theories of messianic time and messianic vocation. We might say of Agamben what the dedicatee of *The Time That Remains*, Jacob Taubes, said of himself in his own work on Paul: 'You all know how little interested I am in grand themes that cannot first be drawn through the eye of philology's needle.'[4]

As did his philosophical masters and, as he himself did in his earlier work on Paul and more recent ones such as *The Kingdom and the Glory* (2007), *Altissima povertà* (2011) and *Opus Dei* (2012), Agamben draws in *The Church and the Kingdom* the most fundamental religious questions and themes through the eye of philology's needle. What he sees, for instance, through the seemingly self-evident terms 'parish' and 'sojourn' (and their common Greek root) is a lost calling, a loss of a sense for the idea of time which infused early Christian thought and in which its messianic element was most alive. There is much more that might be said about Agamben's method. For the matter here at hand, however, it suffices to stress the degree to which Agamben moves from paradigmatic figures and terms to treat the largest and most pressing problems of his time.

When viewed as a whole, few aspects of Agamben's thought are so difficult to grasp as the role of theology and few have posed such problems for his readers. Asked why he so frequently returns to religious or theological motifs in his work, Agamben once answered, 'I think that it is only through metaphysical, religious, and theological paradigms that one can truly approach the contemporary—and political—situation.' Agamben's interviewer then asked, 'And how close does one thereby come to the doctrine of a Divinity?' to which Agamben replied:

> My books [. . .] are confrontations with theology. Walter Benjamin once wrote: My relation to theology is like that of blotting paper to ink. The paper absorbs the ink,

but if it were up to the blotting paper, not
a single drop would remain. This is exactly
how things stand with theology. I am completely steeped in theology, and so then
there is no more; all the ink is gone.[5]

In characteristic fashion, Agamben presents the
role of theology in his thought through an enigmatic
figure borrowed from Benjamin. The remark to
which Agamben alludes is from Benjamin's *Arcades
Project* and reads as follows: 'My thinking is to theology what the blotting paper is to ink. The latter is
completely steeped in the former. Were it up to the
blotting paper, nothing that was written would remain [*Mein Denken verhält sich zur Theologie wie das
Löschblatt zur Tinte. Es ist ganz von ihr vollgesogen. Ginge
es aber nach dem Löschblatt, so würde nichts was geschrieben
ist, übrig bleiben*].'[6] In this singular analogy Benjamin
equates the blotting paper to his thinking and theology to ink. If it were up to his thinking (to the blotting paper) there would be no theology (ink) left.

Following the logic of the metaphor, his thinking would fully absorb theology and nothing of it would remain visible on the page. Yet this leaves us with an important question: What are we to make of what *does* remain on the page?

This too is a vast question (and one which I have attempted to answer elsewhere).[7] The relevant point for *The Church and the Kingdom* is that no such problem arises in its case. As Marco Pacioni presciently noted upon its initial publication, *The Church and the Kingdom* represents a departure from Agamben's earlier writing as in it 'philosophy becomes again the handmaiden of theology,' though it does so not merely to provide the logical bases upon which theology can build but, instead, 'questions anew the matter of faith and the meaning of the earthly institution of which it is the guarantor'.[8]

What, we might then ask, is the nature of this question and how legible is it in *The Church and the*

Kingdom? In another early response, the collective *Ou-vroir de Théologie Potentielle* found that Agamben ef-fected 'a strange synthesis' between 'anarchic radicalism' and 'political Augustinianism'.[9] There is no suggestion that Agamben thinks that the Church could or should hold temporal power of the sort Augustine advocated. And while Agamben's assess-ment is sweeping, and extreme, he does not propose either anarchy or some admixture of anarchy and theocracy. That said, the *Ouvroir de Théologie Potentielle*'s response is not so surprising given how radical is Agamben's call. He finds our times characterized by 'states of permanent exception and emergency', and that 'nowhere on earth today is a legitimate power to be found.' He diagnoses what he calls 'an unprece-dented hypertrophy of law' but does not designate an antidote or even a course of treatment. And most sweepingly, and scathingly, he finds the paradigm of our times in a single religious figure: 'hell'.

The best manner in which to address the questions of anarchy and theocracy, as well as to address questions of hope and despair, is the idea with which I will end this afterword—what Agamben calls 'messianic time'. The more closely Agamben looks at the term *paroikousa*, the more clearly he sees messianic time reflected in it. But what is this messianic time— and 'the messianic experience of time' and 'the messianic vocation' he finds corresponding to it? More- over, how might we understand these ideas in conjunction with the thinkers whose thought Agamben develops here? For Benjamin, to conceive of transience and the messianic together is to grasp 'the present as the "now-time" [. . .] charged with splinters of the messianic [*Splitter der messianischen*]'.[10] When Benjamin wrote of messianic time, and when he employed, as he did here, Pauline terms to do so, he meant not the time while one waited for the coming of a Messiah but, instead, a manner of experiencing and acting on what is already present. What is messianic in Benjamin's conception of messianic time, as in Paul before him and Agamben after him, is not what is to come but what is already here. Messianic time rejects a historical dialectic of progress and its logic of deferral; it rejects the positing of the completion of a historical task in an indeterminate future. To many, 'messianic time' suggests waiting for the Messiah to come, redeem mankind and complete human history. Depending on one's viewpoint, this may strike anarchic or theocratic chords. For Agamben, however, messianic time means, as it did for Benjamin, the very opposite of such waiting, and for this reason he places his focus not on the *ultimate* but on the *penultimate*. In *The Church and the Kingdom* he thus speaks of 'a transformation of the experience of the penultimate', and elsewhere remarks that, 'given that messianic time is not another sort of chronological time, living the last things, the ultimate things, means, above all, living the penultimate things.'[11]

Messianic time is, as Agamben stresses midway through his discourse, not one of apocalypse but of immediacy. About this point he is perfectly explicit, noting not only that 'the time of the messiah, for Paul, cannot be a future time' but also that 'the sole possibility we have to truly grasp the present is to conceive of it as the end. That was Benjamin's idea, and his messianism is to be understood above all after this fashion.'[12] For Agamben, Benjamin's messianism, like his own, is an attempt to grasp the potentialities of our present situation. He will thus say that 'the paradigm for the understanding of the present is messianic time.'[13] And it is for this reason that Agamben writes that the messianic time he envisions is one that should be sought not at the millennium but '*now*'.

Notes

1   Aby Warburg, however, never employed it in his
    writing. It first appeared in print under the pen
    of Warburg's friend and colleague E. R. Curtius
    in the published text of the eulogy he gave at
    Warburg's funeral in 1929. It gained wide cur-
    rency nearly 20 years later through the two ref-
    erences made by Curtius in his *Europäische
    Literatur und Lateinisches Mittelalter*. See E. R. Cur-
    tius, *Europäische Literatur und Lateinisches Mittelalter*
    (European Literature and the Latin Middle
    Ages), 11th edn. (Tübingen and Basel: Francke
    Verlag, 1993), pp. 45 and 386.

2   Walter Benjamin, *Gesammelte Schriften* (Rolf Tiede-
    mann and Herman Schweppenhäuser eds)
    (Frankfurt: Suhrkamp, 1974–89), VOL. 1, p. 208.

3   Martin Heidegger, *Holzwege* (Frankfurt: Kloster-
    mann, 1950), p. 54. Available in English as *Off
    the Beaten Track* (Julian Young and Kenneth

Haynes eds and trans) (Cambridge: Cambridge University Press, 2002).

4   Jakob Taubes, *Die politische Theologie des Paulus* (Munich: Wilhelm Fink Verlag, 1993), p. 123.

5   'Der Papst ist ein weltlicher Priester' (The Pope is a Worldy Priest), interview with Abu Bakr Rieger, *Literaturen* (June 2005): 21–5.

6   Benjamin, *Gesammelte Schriften*, VOL. 5, p. 588 (translation modified).

7   See Chapter 10 of Leland de la Durantaye, *Giorgio Agamben: A Critical Introduction* (Stanford, CA: Stanford University Press, 2009), pp. 366–82.

8   Marco Pacioni, 'Agamben: Appello escatologico alla Chiesa' (An Eschatological Appeal to the Church), *Alias*, 11 September 2010: 23.

9   OuThéoPo, 'La Chiesa e il Regno: Una domanda di Giorgio Agamben a una Chiesa persa nel Tempo' (The Church and the Kingdom: Giorgio Agamben's Question to the Church Lost in Time) (2011). Available at: www.out-heopo.net/chiesa-regno.

10 Benjamin, *Gesammelte Schriften*, VOL. 1, p. 704.

11 Giorgio Agamben, 'Contro i profeti della cata-strofe' (Against the Prophets of Catastophe), *Avvenire*, 12 May 2000: 21.

12 Ibid.; 'Das unheilige Leben: Ein Gespräch mit dem italienischen Philosophen Giorgio Agamben' (The Unholy Life: A Discussion with the Italian Philosopher Giorgio Agamben), interview with Hannah Leitgeb and Cornelia Vismann, *Literaturen* 2(1) (2011): 16–21.

13 Agamben, 'Contro i profeti della catastrofe'.

A Note on the Photographs

ALICE ATTIE

The photographs in this body of work revisit paintings that have come down to us from within the art
historical tradition. They are photographs made from
folded and twisted reproductions of paintings in
books. Distortions of their originals, they exacerbate
and strain their images. Each photograph is a fragment of an image that is itself a fragment recalling
something suspended or thwarted. The images often
mark separation, grief or rupture. Some are pleated
in such a way that one sees only the catastrophic
upheavals on the edges or in the instances of falling.
These are moments of emotional poignancy ex-

tracted from the exorbitance of narratives. When the photographs are culled from Christian iconography, they invoke a restlessness lodged within the sacred, an essential and unbearable sense of loss, of being banished from redemptive space. Perhaps, as Agamben identifies the crisis of Messianic time within the Church, one may envision a theatre of human appeals, of appeal upon appeal, each expanding, delaying and increasing a distance and a deferral. One thinks of Walter Benjamin contemplating the repetitive gestus of Kafka's messengers, expelled even from their own expulsion. This would be a place between prayer and denial: a place where the supplicant has no rest, where inwardness and isolation define a liminal space of waiting, an irremediable space which itself stands for the pathos of human longing.